# YOU ATE MY EARS

NATALIYA VITOROVICH

FOR MISHA AND BABA MICA

Idiom (noun)
> *a group of words established by usage as having a meaning not deducible from those of the individual words*

Idioms are like secret codes. To understand an old saying, a catchphrase, a little superstition, you need to have lived somewhere, become accustomed to its culture, and been exposed to its unique linguistic nuances.

Expressions are so ingrained in our daily speech that we rarely think about how they came into existence or why we use them. It's often only when we try to explain them to another person that we realise their complexity – and often their absurdity.

Last summer when I was visiting my grandparents in Belgrade, I came across a book of Serbian idioms. My baba (grandma) and I went through the phrases together, and as she tried to explain their meanings and origins, we found ourselves laughing ("in stitches," "cracking up," "splitting at the sides"). For instance, in Serbia they like to say, "Jutro je pametnije od večeri," meaning, "The morning is smarter than the evening," an expression that perhaps only makes sense if you've ever spent a long evening drinking with a group of Serbs.

I started to think about how understanding the little figures of speech in a language can lead to learning so much about the everyday life and character of a different culture. For instance, in Greek they say "Να πεθάνει η κατσίκα του γείτονα," which translates to, "The neighbour's goat should die." When I asked my Greek friends for a definition of this saying, they found it difficult to summarise concisely. It's something to do with not wanting to be equal or better than your neighbour, but wishing them to come down to your level. Because if you don't have a goat, then why should they? This expression is one of many which conveys the bluntness and dark humour ubiquitous throughout the Balkans and beyond.

This book is the result of my search for the strangest and most surreal expressions from around the world. In the following pages, I have illustrated the direct translations from the original languages, highlighting the hilarity of idiomatic phrases. So, kick up your heels, let your hair down, feast your eyes and have a whale of a time!

Nataliya Vitorovich

**POLISH**
Mieć muchy w nosie

# HAVING FLIES IN YOUR NOSE

To be sulky; to be irritated or annoyed by something

**SERBIAN**

Kao kuvana noga

# LIKE A BOILED FOOT

To describe feeling exhausted or unfulfilled

**FRENCH**

Ne pas être le couteau le plus aiguisé du tiroir

# NOT THE SHARPEST KNIFE IN THE DRAWER

To describe someone dimwitted or lacking intelligence

**MALAYSIAN**
Seperti kacang lupakan kulit

# LIKE A PEANUT THAT FORGETS ITS SHELL

To describe someone who easily forgets where they came from or who has helped them

**SWEDISH**
Även små grytor har öron

# EVEN SMALL POTS HAVE EARS

The kids might hear

**JAPANESE**

高嶺の花

# FLOWER ON A HIGH PEAK

An unobtainable desire or object; something out of one's reach

**HUNGARIAN**

Miért itatod az egereket?

# WHY ARE YOU GIVING DRINKS TO THE MICE?

Why are you crying?

**RUSSIAN**

Вешать лапшу на уши

# TO HANG NOODLES ON THE EARS

To deceive or fool someone

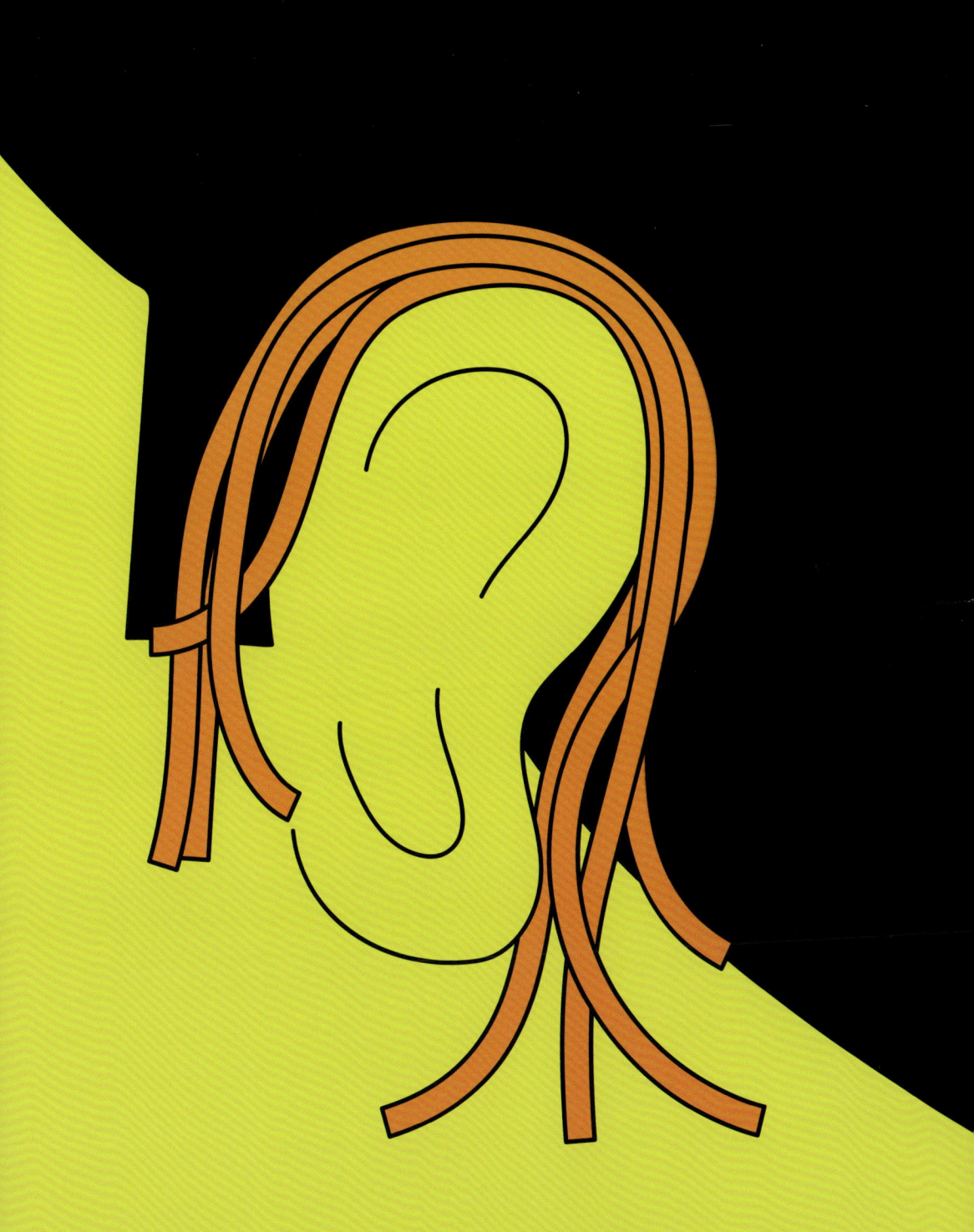

**DANISH**

Er det hestens fødselsdag?

# IS IT THE HORSE'S BIRTHDAY?

The rye bread is too thick on my sandwich

**DUTCH**
Alsof er een engeltje over je tong pist

# AS IF AN ANGEL IS PEEING ON YOUR TONGUE

To describe really enjoying your meal

**INDONESIAN**
Seperti kera mendapat bunga

# LIKE A MONKEY GETTING A FLOWER

To describe a situation where someone gets something unexpectedly or without deserving it

**ARMENIAN**
Գլուխս մի արդուկեր

# STOP IRONING MY HEAD

Stop annoying me

**PORTUGUESE**
Tirar o cavalinho da chuva

# TAKE YOUR LITTLE HORSE AWAY FROM THE RAIN

Give up; move on

**ENGLISH**

# WIND YOUR NECK IN

Mind your own business; calm down

**DANISH**

At have en pind i øret

# TO HAVE A STICK IN YOUR EAR

To be drunk

**TURKISH**

Zemheride yoğurt isteyen, cebinde bir inek taşır

# THOSE WHO WANT YOGHURT IN WINTER MUST CARRY A COW IN THEIR POCKET

To achieve your goals, you have to do what it takes

**PORTUGUESE**
Pagar o pato

# PAY THE DUCK

To take the fall for something

**CZECH**

Jako by hrách na stěnu házel

# LIKE THROWING PEAS AT THE WALL

To describe a situation when the person you are speaking to is not listening

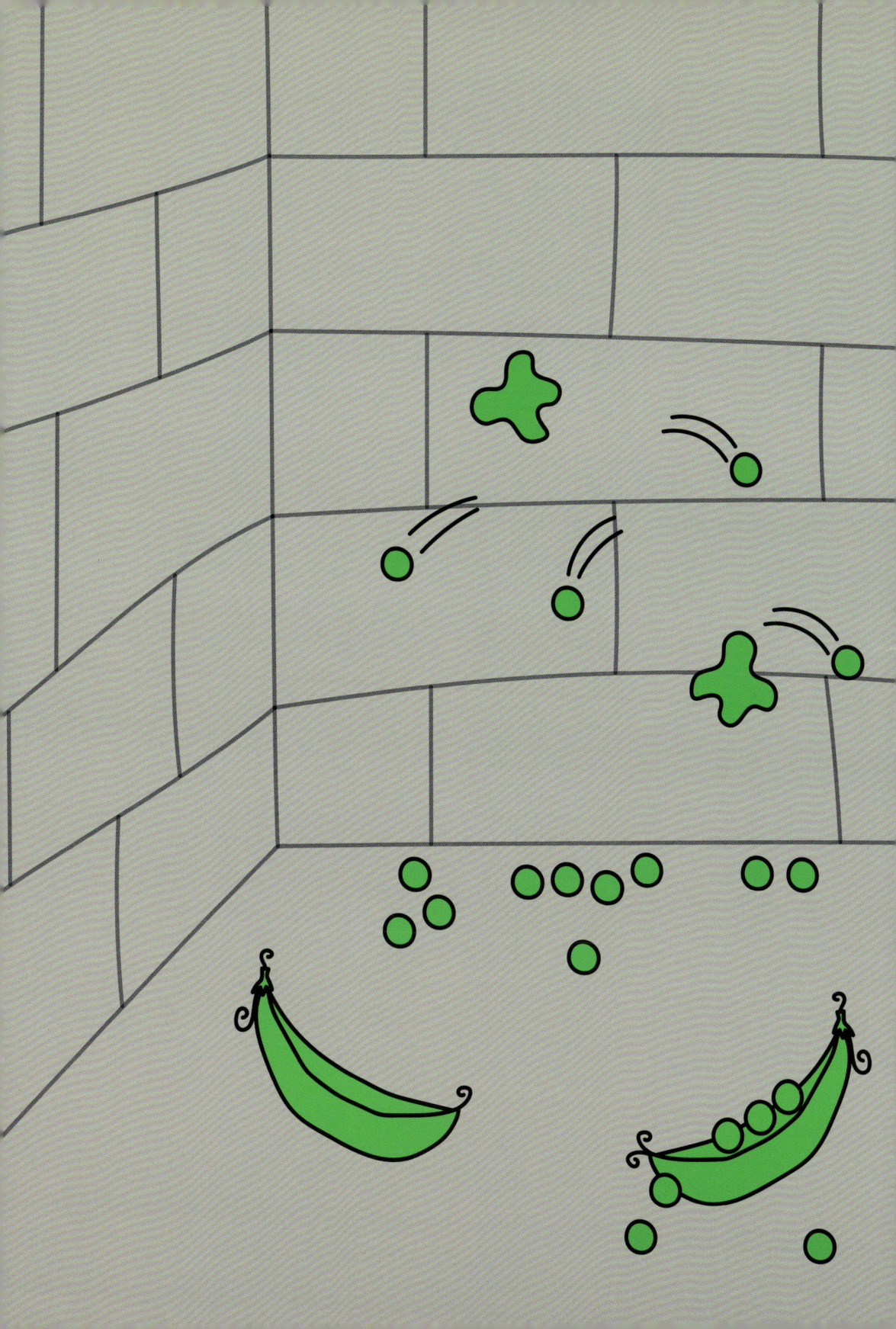

**ARABIC (SYRIA)**

حلّاب النملة

# ANT MILKER

To describe a miserly person; a penny-pincher

**GERMAN**

Wie ein begossener Pudel aussehen

# TO LOOK LIKE A WATERED POODLE

To be ashamed and silent after a criticism, a disappointment or something similar

**SERBIAN**

Ne bacajte bisere pred svinje

# DON'T THROW PEARLS IN FRONT OF A PIG

Don't waste good things on people who will not appreciate them

**GREEK**
Πιάσ' το αβγό και κούρευ' το

# GRAB AN EGG AND GIVE IT A HAIRCUT

To do something difficult, frustrating or pointless

**RUSSIAN**

Когда рак на горе свистнет

# WHEN THE CRAYFISH WHISTLES ON THE MOUNTAIN

To describe something that is most likely never going to happen

**PORTUGUESE**
Alimentar um burro a pão de ló

# TO FEED THE DONKEY SPONGE CAKE

To describe treating someone well who doesn't deserve it

**KOREAN**
수박 겉핥기

# LICKING THE OUTSIDE OF A WATERMELON

To describe superficially experiencing something without delving deeper or fully understanding it

**PORTUGUESE**
Havia de te nascer um pinheiro no cu


MAY A PINE TREE
GROW OUT OF
YOUR BOTTOM


When you wish ill of someone

**GREEK**

Να πεθάνει η κατσίκα του γείτονα

# THE NEIGHBOUR'S GOAT SHOULD DIE

Finding pleasure derived from another person's misfortune

**MANDARIN**

七窍生烟

# TO EMIT SMOKE
# FROM SEVEN ORIFICES

To be extremely angry

**ARMENIAN**
Էշի ականջում քնած լինել

# TO BE ASLEEP IN A DONKEY'S EAR

To describe being out of the loop; missing important news; being uninformed

**JAPANESE**
顔が広い

# TO HAVE A WIDE FACE

To have many friends or be well-connected

**SERBIAN**

Stoji ti ko piletu sise

# IT SUITS YOU LIKE BOOBS WOULD SUIT A CHICKEN

To mock someone; to express that something doesn't suit someone

**SPANISH**

Camarón que se duerme, se lo lleva la corriente

# A SLEEPING PRAWN WILL BE CARRIED AWAY BY THE CURRENT

Used to mean that if you do not pay attention and do something quickly, someone else will do it instead of you

**ENGLISH**

# KICK THE BUCKET

To die

**MANDARIN**
吹牛

# BLOWING THE COW

To boast or brag

**FRENCH**

C'est comme pisser dans un violon

# IT'S LIKE PISSING IN A VIOLIN

To describe making an effort and getting absolutely no result

**GERMAN**

Mit einem lachenden und einem weinenden Auge

# WITH ONE EYE LAUGHING AND ONE EYE CRYING

Having mixed emotions about something

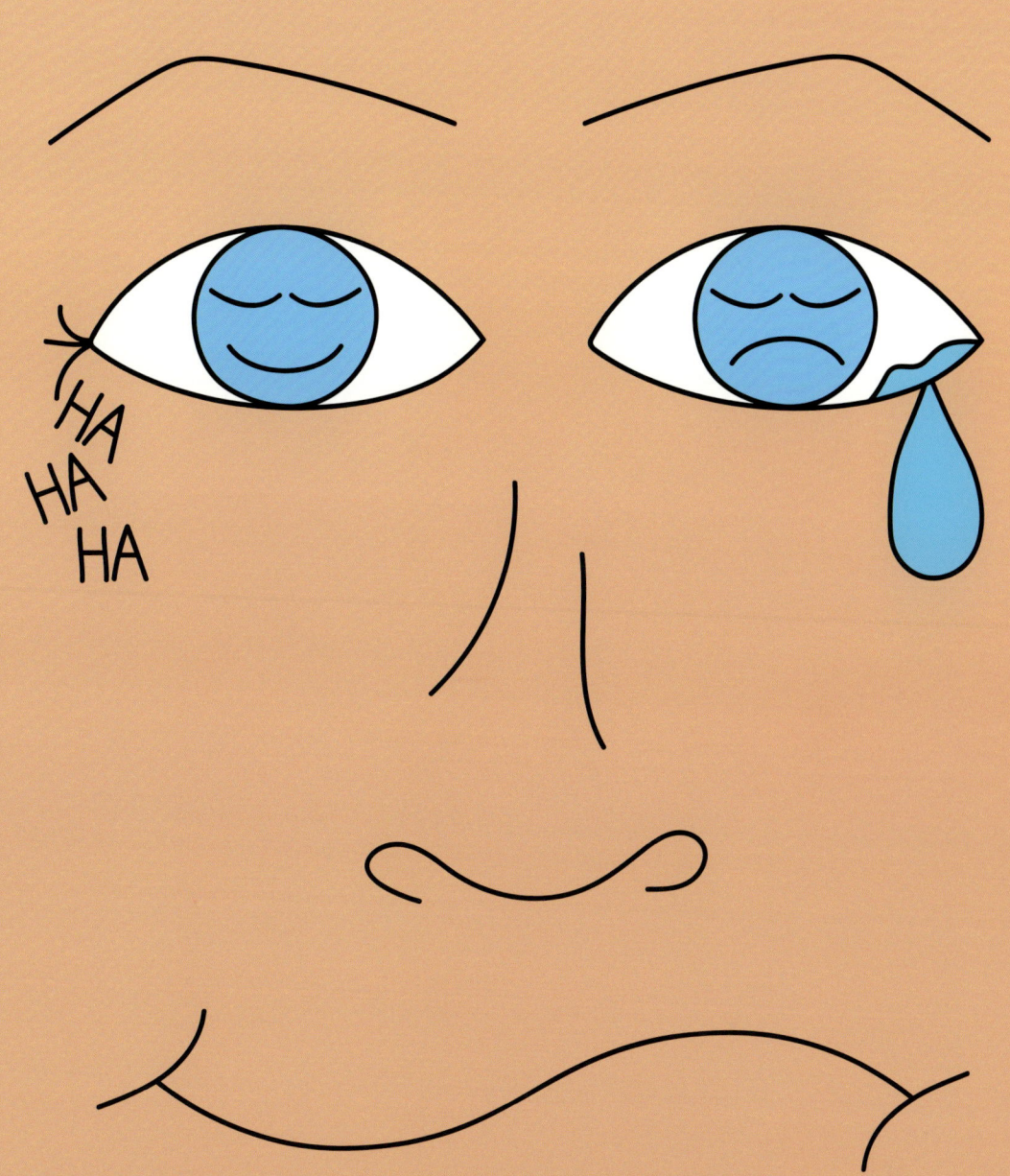

**FARSI**

ماهی ابزار قلزآلات

# A FISH
# WITH SCISSORS

To describe someone who is trying to do too many things at once

**FRENCH**
Péter plus haut que son cul

# TO FART HIGHER
# THAN YOUR BOTTOM

To be stuck up or posh

**DUTCH**

Van een kale kip kan je geen veren plukken

# YOU CAN'T PLUCK FEATHERS FROM A BALD CHICKEN

To describe trying to get something out of nothing

**GREEK**

Μου 'φαγες τα αυτιά

# YOU ATE MY EARS

You are being too loud or talking too much

**FINNISH**

Päästää sammakko suusta

# TO LET A FROG OUT OF YOUR MOUTH

To say the wrong thing

**SWEDISH**
Sitta med skägget i brevlådan

# TO SIT WITH ONE'S BEARD IN THE MAILBOX

To describe being in a difficult situation

**JAPANESE**

花より団子

# DUMPLINGS INSTEAD OF FLOWERS

To describe choosing something useful over something pretty and decorative

**ITALIAN**

Un cane in chiesa

# A DOG IN CHURCH

An unwelcome or unwanted guest

**ARABIC (EGYPT)**

تعصر على نفسك ليمونه

# TO SQUEEZE A LEMON ON YOURSELF

To begrudgingly or reluctantly do something

**ENGLISH**

# TO LEND AN EAR

To listen to someone carefully and sympathetically

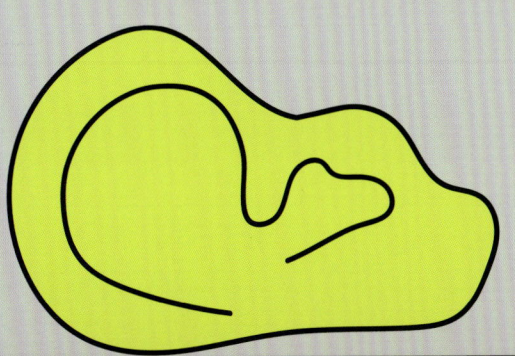

LIBRARY

**AFRIKAANS**

Die koeël is deur die kerk

# THE BULLET WENT THROUGH THE CHURCH

Used when a decision has been made after a long deliberation

**ENGLISH**

# SPARROW'S FART

Very early in the morning

**FLEMISH**

Met uw gat in de boter vallen

# TO FALL WITH YOUR ASS IN THE BUTTER

To be very lucky; to end up in a good place

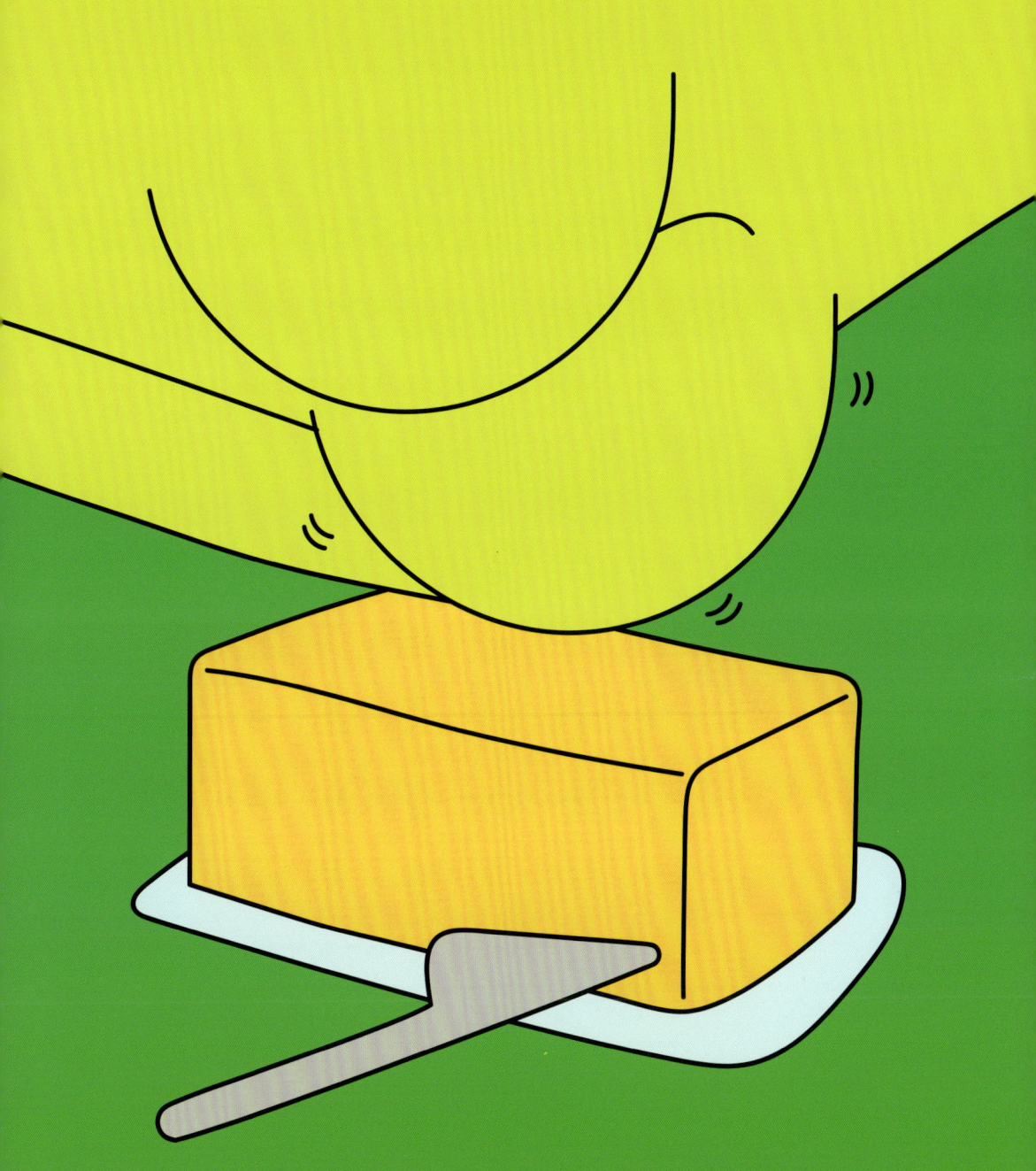

**FRENCH**
Avoir le cul entre deux chaises

# TO HAVE ONE'S ASS BETWEEN TWO CHAIRS

To be undecided; between two options

**GERMAN**

Den Teufel an die Wand malen

# TO DRAW THE DEVIL ON THE WALL

To express that someone is being overly pessimistic or only focused on a worst-case scenario

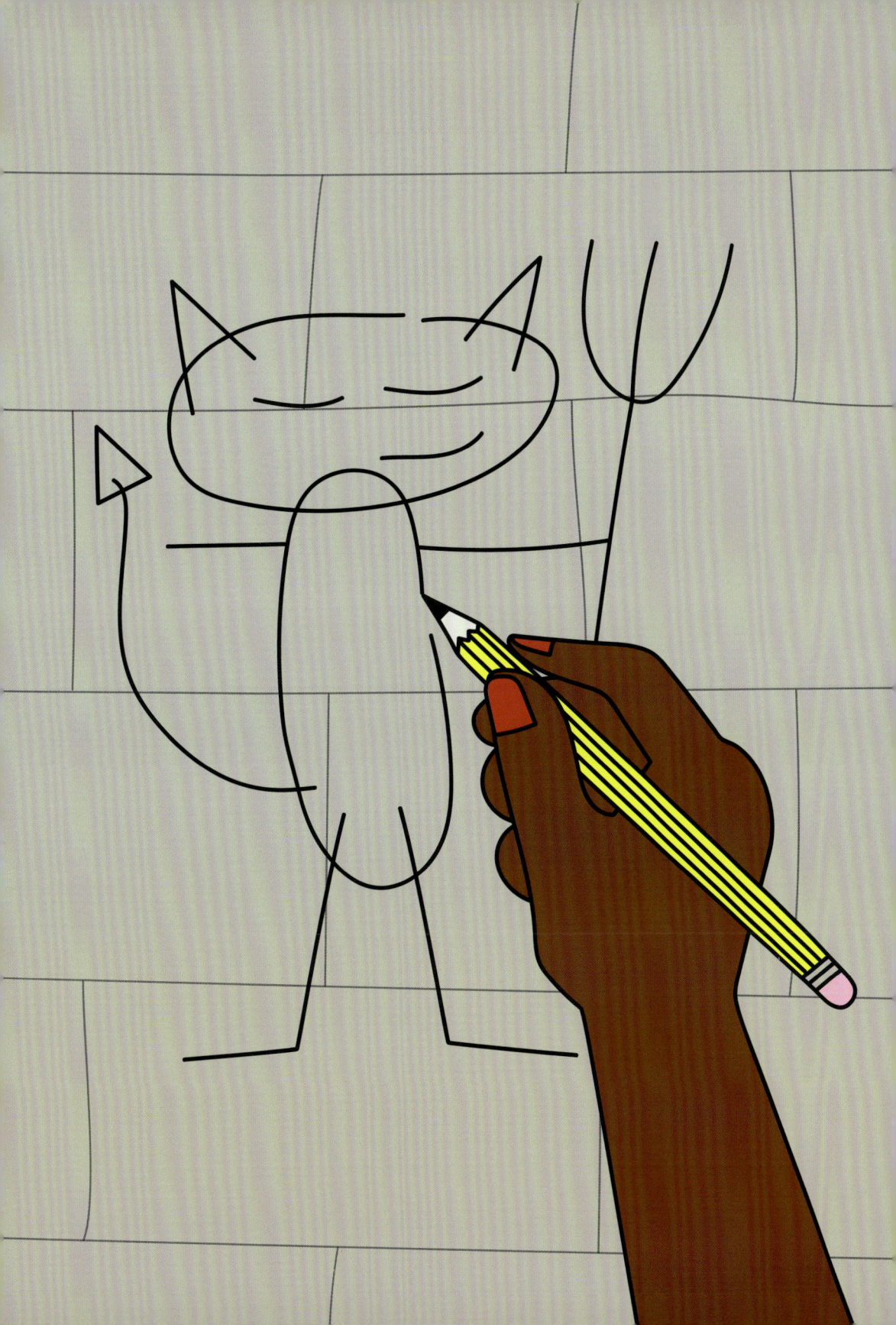

**SWEDISH**

Nu har du skitit i det blå skåpet

# NOW YOU HAVE TAKEN A SHIT IN THE BLUE CUPBOARD

You have made a fool out of yourself

**KOREAN**

남의 떡이 더 커 보인다

# OTHER PEOPLE'S RICE CAKES LOOK BIGGER

To describe the feeling when other people's situations seem better or more attractive than your own

**SPANISH**

Más serio que perro en bote

# MORE SERIOUS THAN A DOG IN A BOAT

To describe someone who is very serious or nervous, often due to fear or discomfort

**ICELANDIC**

Rúsínan í pylsuendanum

# THE RAISIN AT THE END OF THE HOT DOG

To describe a pleasant surprise or the highlight of a day or experience

**SPANISH**

Estirando el chicle

# STRETCHING THE CHEWING GUM

Making things go on longer than they should; holding onto something that is no longer important

**FRENCH**

Arriver comme un cheveu sur la soupe

# TO ARRIVE LIKE A HAIR IN THE SOUP

Referring to an irrelevant or out-of-context remark;
an unwanted or unexpected guest

**ICELANDIC**
Að tefla við páfann

# PLAYING CHESS WITH THE POPE

To have a poo

**ENGLISH**

# TO HAVE A CHIP ON YOUR SHOULDER

To have an unpleasant attitude caused by the belief that one has been treated unfairly in the past

**ROMANIAN**

A călca pe bec

# TO STEP ON A LIGHT BULB

To become pregnant

Thank you firstly to my dear friend Mo, who gave me invaluable feedback throughout the making of this book… I'm eternally grateful for your patience and honesty.

A big, big thank you to Andreas and Stathis for making this publication possible and for your encouragement, support and enthusiasm.

A massive thank you to everyone that sent me idioms, and to all those who spell checked the original languages.

And lastly, a special mention to my sister Valentina and my brother Maxim, my Deda (grandpa) Mile, and my dad Sacha, who always encouraged me to make a book.

YOU ATE MY EARS
by Nataliya Vitorovich

Published by
Hyper Hypo

Printed by
Kostopoulos Printing

May 2024
1.000 copies

©2024, Hyper Hypo
for this edition

©2024, Nataliya Vitorovich
for her drawings and text

www.hyperhypo.gr